Noël and Sherlock

by Brenda Short

This is a work of fiction. Any reference to people, places or events are creations of the author's imagination and any resemblance to actual events, places or persons living or dead is entirely coincidental.

Library and Archives Canada Cataloguing in Publication

ISBN 978-1-0691530-3-6 (pbk)

Short, Brenda, author

Noël and Sherlock / Brenda Short

Illustrated by Microsoft AI

Published by Doonhamer Publishing

2nd edition 2024

Dedication

To Julie Fox, tech wizard, my eternal gratitude for her assistance with this project and many others.

Preface

This is a fictitious story about a young boy, Noël Holmes and his dog, Sherlock.

Ruth is home alone and missing her family. Christmas is approaching, but the airport has been closed down because of a winter storm, preventing her family from joining her, and so she has to spend the holiday alone.

Then out of the blue, she is visited by a charming boy and his little dog.

Children's books by this author

1. The Cherry Pie Incident
2. Noël and Sherlock
3. I'll Fix That Cat Later!
4. The Christmas Surprise
5. Frank's My Name
6. The Empty Nest
7. Easter Bunny Has a Fever
8. The Fishing Trip

Noël and Sherlock

The phone rang just as Ruth emerged from the shower. She grabbed her towel and rushed through to the bedroom, dripping water everywhere.

There was an apologetic voice on the other end of the phone.

Of course, she had known it was her son before she answered and she had a sinking feeling in the pit of her stomach that she would be alone for Christmas.

It had been snowing and blowing for two days now and there was no sign of it letting up.

"Sorry mum," he said. "They cancelled our flight and we can't re-route through New York. Seems like the storm is affecting half the province. No flights in or out of Pearson Airport and no trains either." Ruth had been so looking forward to this visit from her son and his family, but Mother Nature wasn't cooperating.

Everyone wanted a white Christmas for sentimental reasons, but there was no denying that this was too much snow.

"Not to worry, it can't be helped. We can catch up later – maybe for New Year," she said bravely.

The smile in her voice hid her disappointment as they said their goodbyes.

Sometime after lunch, Ruth decided to decorate the tree. This was something she had hoped to be doing this evening with her grandchildren, but now they wouldn't be there to help her.

Of course, she could do it herself, although it wouldn't be the same, but she so loved the tree and without it, it wouldn't feel like Christmas.

Then there were piles of presents in the corner that she had spent the best part of yesterday wrapping to put underneath the tree, and complete the effect.

Three hours later, Ruth poured herself a cup of tea and sat back to gaze at her handiwork.

The finishing touches were completed and the tree dominated the family room in its magnificence, the lights showing to best advantage as always in the advancing dusk.

As soon as darkness fell, there was a very faint knock at the door. Ruth almost missed it, but then, there it was again, an insistent tapping.

When she opened the door, she discovered to her amazement a young boy standing on the doorstep, and looking very cold.

"Can I come inside please?" he asked.

She looked around but couldn't see anyone else. "Where are your parents? Who are you with?" she said warily.

Ruth was alone in the house, so she had to be concerned for her safety, but there was nobody in sight, so she brought him inside.

"Let's go into the kitchen and make some hot chocolate," she coaxed, removing his snow encrusted jacket, "What's your name?"

“My name is Noël! I don’t know where my mama is,” he said, holding her hand tightly as he walked beside her.

His tiny hand was so cold. Her maternal instincts flared up suddenly.

How on earth did he end up in that storm, with nobody to protect him? Where was his family?

Ruth attempted to contact the local police, to tell them about the boy in case people were out looking for him. She wanted to let them know that he was safe, but there was no dial tone on her house phone. The lines must be down.

She picked up her cell phone, but there was no service their either. So, she gave up trying for now and brought out some food leftover from lunch, but Noël just picked at it, more content with the hot chocolate.

They went through to the family room, and he sat on the cushion in the corner of the hearth in full view of the Christmas tree, with twinkling lights reflecting in his bright, blue eyes.

That old cushion had been there when she bought the house and for some unknown reason, she had kept it. It just seemed to belong there.

Ruth sat down in her rocking chair and picked up a particular story book.

This was a Christmas tradition that began years before, and was meant for her grandchildren, but instead, she would share it with this little, lost soul, rescued from the storm.

She began to read the story to Noël. It had been her son's favourite Christmas story about a little boy who asked Santa for a puppy, but didn't have a name for it.

The story invited the reader to choose the puppy's name.

"What would you like to call the dog?" asked Ruth.

"I have a dog. His name is Sherlock.

Can we call the dog Sherlock?" asked the lad.

So, Ruth continued the story about a little boy named Noël who got a puppy for Christmas, then lost his way in a snow storm, but his puppy, Sherlock found him and brought him home.

Noël eventually began to yawn and Ruth decided it was time for bed.

She took one of the Christmas presents from under the tree and unwrapped it to reveal a set of pyjamas. She had bought these for her youngest grandson.

He was about the same age as Noël and they fitted perfectly.

As soon as she tucked him in, he fell sound asleep. It had been wonderful having a young child to care for again, but this one was surrounded by mystery.

Nobody had come to her door looking for him. Where were his parents? Had something happened to them in the storm?

Ruth attempted to get through on the phone once more without success. She would try again first thing.

In the morning, Ruth went in to wake the child, but there was nobody in the bed.

The only indication that he had ever been there was a slight depression in the pillow and the pyjamas that he wore, neatly folded.

She searched the house, but there was no sign of him.

Eventually she managed to contact the local police and report to them that she found a child on her doorstep, but that somehow, he had disappeared.

Was she losing her mind, she wondered? However, a little while later, a police officer arrived.

He said he had a strange story to tell her, about a tragedy that happened just outside of town 80 years before.

Ruth busied herself making coffee for both of them and he sat down at the kitchen table.

"As the story goes, according to the old timers that hang around at the general store," he began, "there was a train wreck hereabouts, just before Christmas...in a wooded area, maybe two miles or so west of town.

“A small boy called Noël Holmes became separated from his parents, when the train they were travelling in hit a fallen tree and went off the rails.

They say the child was probably disoriented and wandered off in the middle of a blizzard.

“He had a dog, no more than a pup, and it was howling incessantly in the baggage compartment trying to dig its way out of the holding cage.

As soon as they let it out of its cage it ran off, struggling through the deep snow.”

He stopped for a moment to sip his coffee, complimenting her on the taste, warming his hands on the cup as if he was imagining the storm.

“They searched all night for the boy and his dog, and eventually found them, lying beside each other, so close to their house.”

He paused for effect, watching for her reaction before continuing.

"The dog's name was Sherlock, named ironically after Sherlock Holmes, and the family lived at 15 Plumtree Lane."

"But that's…that's my address," said Ruth amazed.

"Oh yes! And I almost forgot to tell you…the boy and the dog have been known to come back and visit sometimes, at Christmas," he said laughing, "but only when there's a big snowstorm."

The officer stayed for a while, realizing that Ruth was alone and might appreciate some company on Christmas Day.

He was enjoying his coffee with her, and the telling of the local folklore, but eventually he had to go back to work.

Just after the officer took his leave and drove off, Ruth heard barking and scratching at the door, and when she opened it, there stood the cutest little beagle wagging his tail furiously.

He barked again and then came running inside, with long ears flapping, and a pink tongue hanging out one side of his mouth.

"Oh no! Just a minute. Come back little dog," she called, failing to stop him from coming inside.

He made a beeline for the old cushion on the hearth, sniffing it thoroughly as if he recognized a familiar scent.

He seemed to know the cushion would be there and lay down, claiming it as his prize as he continued to wag his tail.

Ruth closed the front door purposefully and walked through to the family room to retrieve the dog, but now there was no sign of him.

“He came in here…I saw him, I’m sure of it!” she said out loud.

But what was that? There, laying on the floor beside the cushion, was a brand new leather collar with a silver dog tag.

The beagle had evaporated it seemed, or was she imagining the whole thing?

Ruth picked it up, but she already knew what she would find.

On one side the name Sherlock was inscribed. She turned it over, and gasped. 15 Plumtree Lane, 1938…

The phone rang suddenly, startling her. It was Washington, D.C.

“Hello mum, it’s just me. Merry Christmas!” said her son, with a background chorus of little people joining in.

“We should be able to catch a flight tomorrow. How was your Christmas so far? Anything interesting…?”

“You have no idea,” she said, fascinated for a moment as the collar slowly faded away and she was left holding nothing but her Christmas fantasy…

“I think I’m going to get myself a dog…and call him Sherlock!”

www.ingramcontent.com/pod-product-compliance
Lightning Source LLC
LaVergne TN
LVHW021352160826
845679LV00008B/1596

* 9 7 8 1 0 6 9 1 5 3 0 3 6 *